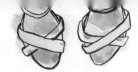

January 1

The godly woman faces her challenges
with prayer, a sense of adventure,
and a great pair of boots.

December 31

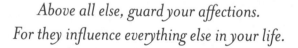

Above all else, guard your affections.
For they influence everything else in your life.

PROVERBS 4:23

5-20-2020

To:

HATLEY

From:

PAPA & BETSY

WE LOVE YOU!

WALK BY FAITH

Cover Scripture from the New King James Version.
Copyright © 1982 by Thomas Nelson, Inc.

© The Living Bible. Taken from the Living Bible
with permission from Tyndale House Publishers, Inc., Wheaton, IL.

Scripture taken from The Holy Bible, New International Version® NIV®.
© 1973, 1978, 1984 by International Bible Society.
Used by permission of Zondervan.

Made in China

January 2

What a wonderful God we have—
He is the Father of our Lord Jesus Christ,
the source of every mercy.

II CORINTHIANS 1:3, 4

December 30

Keep traveling steadily along His pathway
and in due season He will
honor you with every blessing.

PSALM 37:34

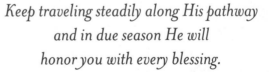

January 3

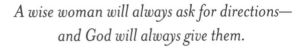

A wise woman will always ask for directions—
and God will always give them.

December 29

*She was comfortable in her own shoes,
and she discovered they looked best
with the uniqueness God had given her.*

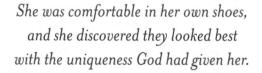

January 4

If you want to know what God wants you to do,
ask Him, and He will gladly tell you.

JAMES 1:5

December 28

All who humble themselves before the Lord
shall be given every blessing,
and shall have wonderful peace.

PSALM 37:11

January 5

*The best form of exercise
has nothing to do with equipment—
and everything to do with faith.*

December 27

She is a woman of strength and dignity,
and has no fear of old age.

PROVERBS 31:25

January 6

Spend your time and energy
in the exercise of keeping spiritually fit.

I TIMOTHY 4:7

December 26

It was time to put on a new hat—
the one stitched together
with hope and courage.

January 7

Trials build patience, make us strong,
and teach us that sometimes,
prayer and truffles do *go together.*

December 25

These will be His royal titles:
"Wonderful," "Counselor,"
"The Mighty God,"
"The Everlasting Father,"
"The Prince of Peace."

ISAIAH 9:6

January 8

When your patience is finally in full bloom,
then you will be ready for anything,
strong in character, full and complete.

JAMES 1:4

December 24

*I bring you the most joyful news
ever announced...the Savior—yes,
the Messiah, the Lord—has been born.*

LUKE 2:10, 11

January 9

When God asks you to step out of
your comfort zone, do it—
and wear a glorious pair of shoes.

December 23

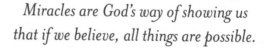

*Miracles are God's way of showing us
that if we believe, all things are possible.*

January 10

When I am afraid,
I will put my confidence in You.

PSALM 56:3

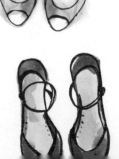

December 22

I will sing to the Lord
because He has blessed me so richly.

PSALM 13:6

January 11

*God wants to use you to adorn
the world with His beauty—no matter
what kind of hair day you're having!*

December 21

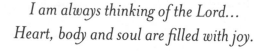

I am always thinking of the Lord...
Heart, body and soul are filled with joy.

PSALM 16:8, 9

January 12

May you always be doing those good,
kind things that show
you are a child of God.

PHILIPPIANS 1:11

December 20

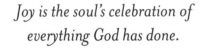

*Joy is the soul's celebration of
everything God has done.*

January 13

Hope!
It will keep you looking incredibly young.

December 19

God Himself is blessing you forever.

PSALM 45:2

January 14

*Hope will keep you
happy and full of peace.*

ROMANS 15:13

December 18

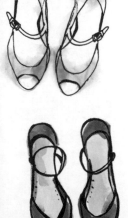

*Fill all who love You
with Your happiness.*

PSALM 5:11

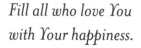

January 15

God saw to every detail,
and her character grew
more and more beautiful.

December 17

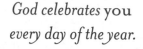

*God celebrates you
every day of the year.*

January 16

Lord, You are our Father.
We are the clay and You are the Potter.
We are all formed by Your hand.

ISAIAH 64:8

December 16

God's Son shines out with God's glory.

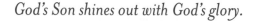

HEBREWS 1:3

January 17

Hold tightly to your faith,
even when there's no chocolate in sight.

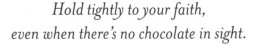

December 15

Where is the newborn King?...
for we have seen His star...
and have come to worship Him.

MATTHEW 2:2

January 18

What is faith?
It is the confident assurance that
something we want is going to happen.

HEBREWS 11:1

December 14

She loved to gaze at the stars in the sky,
for they gleamed with the majesty
of the One who created them.

January 19

Put on comfortable shoes and
head in the direction of your dreams—
God has prepared the path ahead of you.

December 13

Let us walk in the light of the Lord.

ISAIAH 2:5

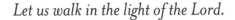

January 20

Be strong!
Be courageous!
Do not be afraid!...
For the Lord your God will be with you.

DEUTERONOMY 31:6

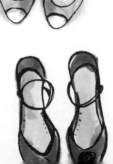

December 12

Let your good deeds glow for all to see,
so that they will praise your heavenly Father.

MATTHEW 5:16

January 21

Joy is strength,
and laughter is a little
pick-me-up for the soul.

December 11

She was absolutely glowing in her fashionable red dress, sparkly earrings, and passion for God.

January 22

The joy of the Lord is your strength.

NEHEMIAH 8:10

December 10

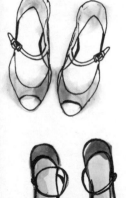

He sends the snow in all its lovely whiteness,
and scatters the frost upon the ground.

PSALM 147:16

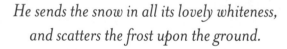

January 23

*We can do great things if we
focus on the great God who created us!*

December 9

Decorate your life with God's love.

January 24

*The people who know their God
shall be strong and do great things.*

DANIEL 11:32

December 8

Everything comes from God alone.

ROMANS 11:36

January 25

*Make the most of the opportunities
God gives you to shine today.*

December 7

Through Christ,
all the kindness of God
has been poured out upon us.

ROMANS 1:5

January 26

Those who are wise—the people of God—
shall shine as brightly as the sun's brilliance.

DANIEL 12:3

December 6

The most fashionable coat we will ever wear
is one made of kindness and love.

January 27

Who needs a facelift when God's word can renew the spirit, soul, **and** *body!*

December 5

I am on my way to heaven;
I belong to Christ.

I JOHN 2:4

January 28

You have been chosen by God
who has given you this new kind of life.

COLOSSIANS 3:12

December 4

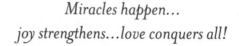

Miracles happen…
joy strengthens…love conquers all!

January 29

God knows how to pack the good stuff into our day, our week, our year—even if our attitude gets a little wrinkled at times.

December 3

Our light is from Your light.
Pour out Your unfailing love
on those who know You!

PSALM 36:9, 10

January 30

*A woman of enthusiasm is glorious to see—
and glorious to be!*

December 2

Her heart believed…
and she sparkled from head to toe.

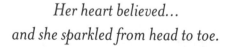

January 31

Work hard and cheerfully at all you do,
just as though you were working for the Lord.

COLOSSIANS 3:23

December 1

*God showed His great love for us
by sending Christ.*

ROMANS 5:8

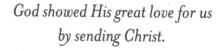

February 1

Everything comes from God alone.

ROMANS 11:36

November 30

Amazing Thought #37:
*You are loved and cared for
every moment by the God who
holds the universe in His hands.*

February 2

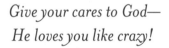

Give your cares to God—
He loves you like crazy!

November 29

How we thank You, Lord!
Your mighty miracles
give proof that You care.

PSALM 75:1

February 3

Let Him have all your worries and cares,
for He is always thinking about you
and watching everything that concerns you.

I PETER 5:7

November 28

Come before Him with thankful hearts.

PSALM 95:2

February 4

*There's more happiness in a single moment
of God's presence than in anything else in life
(and He doesn't mind if you sweeten the
happy moments with a little chocolate).*

November 27

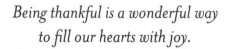

*Being thankful is a wonderful way
to fill our hearts with joy.*

February 5

*You have let me experience
the joys of life and the exquisite pleasures
of Your own eternal presence.*

PSALM 16:11

November 26

Sing praises to the Lord!
Raise your voice in song to Him
who rides upon the clouds.

PSALM 68:4

February 6

Go after your dreams—
God created you to live them!

November 25

Your power and goodness, Lord,
reach to the highest heavens.
You have done such wonderful things.

PSALM 71:19

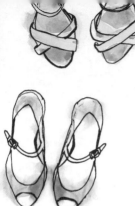

February 7

When dreams come true at last,
there is life and joy.

PROVERBS 13:12

November 24

Lord, let my life be a continual melody
of thankfulness to You!

February 8

*She loved the Lord with all her heart,
and it cast an amazing light
on everything she did.*

November 23

Your own soul is nourished
when you are kind.

PROVERBS 11:17

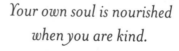

February 9

God looked over all that He had made,
and it was excellent in every way.

GENESIS 1:31

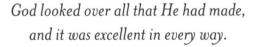

November 22

*May my spoken words and unspoken thoughts
be pleasing even to You, O Lord.*

PSALM 19:14

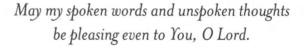

February 10

*Every woman should have
a mirror that reflects her spirit—
that's where God brings out her true beauty.*

November 21

*Words are such
important things to be careful with.*

February 11

*Be beautiful inside, in your hearts,
with the lasting charm of a gentle and
quiet spirit that is so precious to God.*

I PETER 3:4

November 20

When she speaks,
her words are wise,
and kindness is the rule
for everything she says.

PROVERBS 31:26

February 12

*She welcomes the years with
arms open wide and loves life with the kind
of passion that comes straight from God.*

November 19

Those who use God's wisdom are safe.

PROVERBS 28:26

February 13

Rejoice in every day of life.

ECCLESIASTES 11:8

November 18

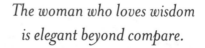

The woman who loves wisdom
is elegant beyond compare.

February 14

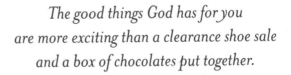

*The good things God has for you
are more exciting than a clearance shoe sale
and a box of chocolates put together.*

November 17

Always be thankful.

COLOSSIANS 3:15

February 15

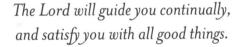

The Lord will guide you continually,
and satisfy you with all good things.

ISAIAH 58:11

November 16

*Remind each other
of God's goodness and be thankful.*

EPHESIANS 5:4

February 16

Be inspired. Be brave.
Be YOU!

November 15

She thought about everything
she wanted to say to God,
and it always started with,
"Thank You."

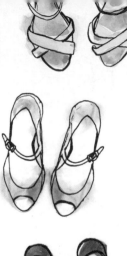

February 17

Your workmanship is marvelous—
and how well I know it.
You were there while I was
being formed in utter seclusion!

PSALM 139:14, 15

November 14

He is like a Father to us,
tender and sympathetic.

PSALM 103:13

February 18

She LIVES.
She LOVES.
She LAUGHS.
She makes every day
a celebration of who she is in Christ.

November 13

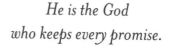

He is the God
who keeps every promise.

PSALM 146:6

February 19

*Because of what Christ
has done, we have become
gifts to God that He delights in.*

EPHESIANS 1:11

November 12

Head up, shoulders back,
thoughts positive,
heart set on the promises of God.

February 20

*Be fabulous—God spared
no enthusiasm when He created you!*

November 11

The lovingkindness of the Lord
is from everlasting to everlasting.

PSALM 103:17

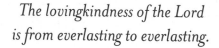

February 21

*Thank You for making me
so wonderfully complex!
It is amazing to think about.*

PSALM 139:14

November 10

God loves you **no matter what.**

February 22

She's the kind of person who
looks at a cloud and says to herself,
"There's a rainbow coming in just a little while."
Then she kicks off her shoes and
dances in the puddles until
the sun comes out again.

November 9

In everything you do,
put God first,
and He will direct you.

PROVERBS 3:6

February 23

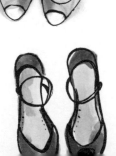

"For I know the plans I have for you,"
says the Lord. "They are plans for good."

JEREMIAH 29:11

November 8

God is in control—let go!

February 24

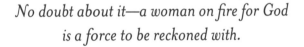

*No doubt about it—a woman on fire for God
is a force to be reckoned with.*

November 7

Trust the Lord completely.

PROVERBS 3:5

February 25

Love the Lord and follow His plan for your lives.
Cling to Him and serve Him enthusiastically.

JOSHUA 22:5

November 6

God,
who knows all hearts,
knows yours.

PROVERBS 24:12

February 26

In hard times she had learned three things—
she was stronger than she ever imagined,
Jesus was closer than she ever realized,
and she was loved more than she ever knew.

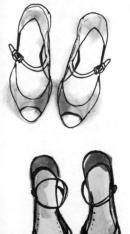

November 5

The heart is a fragile thing,
it can't be trusted to just anyone.
Thank goodness God isn't just anyone.

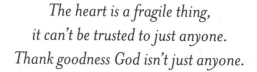

February 27

God loves you very much...don't be afraid!
Calm yourself; be strong—yes, strong!

DANIEL 10:19

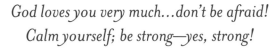

November 4

How great He is!
His power is absolute!
His understanding is unlimited.

PSALM 147:5

February 28

*Her spirit loved to bask
in the brightness of her future.*

November 3

You are merciful and gentle, Lord,
slow in getting angry,
full of constant lovingkindness.

PSALM 86:15

February 29

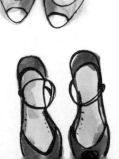

A bright future lies ahead!

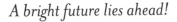

PROVERBS 24:14

November 2

*With such an enormous amount of stuff
to be learned, there are a million reasons
to thank God for being patient with us.*

March 1

*A woman armed with chocolate
and a prayer partner needs little else
to get through the day.*

November 1

Lord, with all my heart I thank You.

PSALM 138:1

March 2

If two of you agree down here on earth
concerning anything you ask for,
my Father in heaven will do it for you.

MATTHEW 18:19

October 31

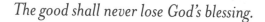

The good shall never lose God's blessing.

PROVERBS 10:30

March 3

You are bright and gifted—
you are a woman of God.

October 30

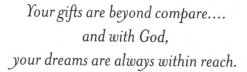

Your gifts are beyond compare....
and with God,
your dreams are always within reach.

March 4

*Your greatest glory will
be that you belong to Him.*

II THESSALONIANS 1:12

October 29

God blesses those who obey Him.

PROVERBS 16:20

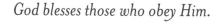

March 5

Wisdom in three words:
Lord help me!

October 28

We can make our plans,
but the final outcome is in God's hands.

PROVERBS 16:1

March 6

In my distress I screamed
to the Lord for His help.
And He heard me from heaven.

PSALM 18:6

October 27

Open your heart to God,
and life will open the doors to your dreams.

March 7

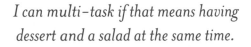

I can multi-task if that means having dessert and a salad at the same time.

October 26

If you search for good,
you will find God's favor.

PROVERBS 11:27

March 8

*A cheerful heart
does good like medicine.*

PROVERBS 17:22

October 25

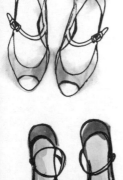

Do you want to be truly rich?
You already are if you are happy and good.

I TIMOTHY 6:6

March 9

It really is all about love.
God says so.

October 24

She knew the day would bring
opportunities to make God smile,
and she would happily take each one of them.

March 10

*Pay all your debts except the debt of love
for others—never finish paying that!*

ROMANS 13:8

October 23

Wisdom is a fountain of life.

PROVERBS 16:22

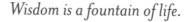

March 11

Love the Lord your God
with all your heart, soul, and mind.

MATTHEW 22:37

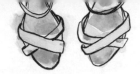

October 22

I will praise the Lord no matter what happens.
I will constantly speak of His glories and grace.

PSALM 34:1

March 12

Sit quietly.
Breathe deeply.
Hope steadily.
God is working on your behalf
this very moment.

October 21

There are some days when
you just have to hang the 'Be Brave' sign
on your heart and dive in!

March 13

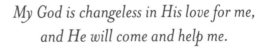

My God is changeless in His love for me,
and He will come and help me.

PSALM 59:10

October 20

Every morning tell Him,
"Thank You for Your kindness,"
and every evening
rejoice in all His faithfulness.

PSALM 92:2

March 14

I will tell everyone how good You are,
and of Your constant, daily care.
I walk in the strength of the Lord.

PSALM 71:15, 16

October 19

He is good to everyone, and His compassion is intertwined with everything He does.

PSALM 145:9

March 15

God told her anything is possible,
so she lived her life
believing it with all her heart.

October 18

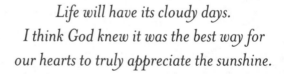

*Life will have its cloudy days.
I think God knew it was the best way for
our hearts to truly appreciate the sunshine.*

March 16

With God everything is possible.

MARK 10:27

October 17

*Love each other
just as much as I love you.*

JOHN 13:34

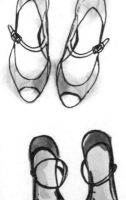

March 17

You love me so much!
You are constantly so kind!

PSALM 86:13

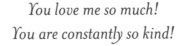

October 16

May your roots go down deep into the soil
of God's marvelous love.

EPHESIANS 3:17

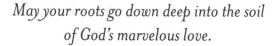

March 18

Be good to yourself.
God only made one of you!

October 15

*Life is all about loving God and loving others—
it really is as simple as that.*

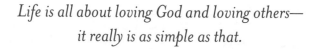

March 19

Turn to Him so He can...
send you wonderful times of refreshment
from the presence of the Lord.

ACTS 3:19

October 14

When the Holy Spirit controls our lives
He will produce this kind of fruit in us:
love, joy, peace, patience, kindness, goodness,
faithfulness, gentleness and self-control.

GALATIANS 5:22, 23

March 20

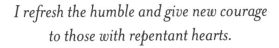

*I refresh the humble and give new courage
to those with repentant hearts.*

ISAIAH 57:15

October 13

*Moods have a way of swinging
just when you need them to hold still—
and there's one word for that:*
pray.

March 21

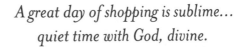

A great day of shopping is sublime…
quiet time with God, divine.

October 12

Lord...
I am looking up to You in constant hope.

PSALM 86:3

March 22

You have let me experience the joys of life
and the exquisite pleasures
of Your own eternal presence.

PSALM 16:11

October 11

*I will meditate about Your glory,
splendor, majesty and miracles.*

PSALM 145:5

March 23

*Friendship with God is reserved
for those who reverence Him.
With them alone He shares
the secrets of His promises.*

PSALM 25:14

October 10

A great pair of heels can't solve everything…
but they do lift you a teensy bit closer to God.

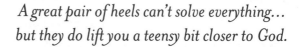

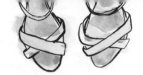

March 24

She knew there would be bumps in the road,
so she protected her heart,
adjusted her attitude, and held onto
God's promises with both hands.

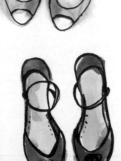

October 9

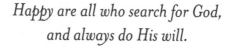

Happy are all who search for God,
and always do His will.

PSALM 119:2

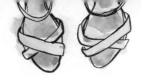

March 25

He will shield you with His wings!
They will shelter you.
His faithful promises are your armor.

PSALM 91:4

October 8

Be happy. Grow in Christ.
Live in harmony and peace.

II CORINTHIANS 13:11

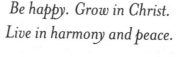

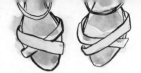

March 26

*Open your arms wide
and let God bless you!*

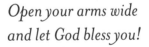

October 7

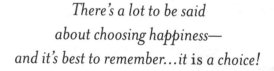

*There's a lot to be said
about choosing happiness—
and it's best to remember...it is a choice!*

March 27

You will receive every blessing you can use!

PSALM 81:10

October 6

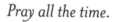

Pray all the time.

EPHESIANS 6:18

March 28

Those who trust the Lord
shall be given every blessing.

PSALM 37:9

October 5

Talk with each other much about the Lord.

EPHESIANS 5:19

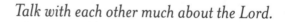

March 29

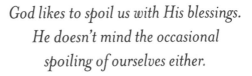

God likes to spoil us with His blessings.
He doesn't mind the occasional
spoiling of ourselves either.

October 4

Live. Laugh. Love. Pray.
P R A I S E.
Every day!

March 30

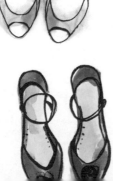

*Happy are those who are
strong in the Lord, who want above all else
to follow Your steps.*

PSALM 84:5

October 3

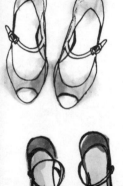

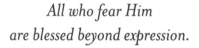

All who fear Him
are blessed beyond expression.

PSALM 112:1

March 31

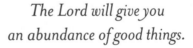

*The Lord will give you
an abundance of good things.*

DEUTERONOMY 28:11

October 2

If we're going to be enthusiastic about life,
we must be passionate about God.

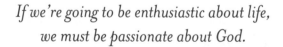

April 1

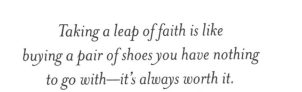

*Taking a leap of faith is like
buying a pair of shoes you have nothing
to go with—it's always worth it.*

October 1

We meditate upon
Your kindness and Your love.

PSALM 48:9

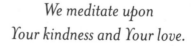

April 2

*These trials are only to test your faith,
to see whether or not it is strong and pure.*

1 PETER 1:7

September 30

In silence and stillness,
your spirit can dream.

April 3

*Today's beauty secret: contentment—
it's great for the soul's complexion.*

September 29

*Wisdom and truth will enter
the very center of your being,
filling your life with joy.*

PROVERBS 2:10

April 4

I have learned the
secret of contentment in every situation.

PHILIPPIANS 4:12

September 28

O God, my heart is quiet and confident.

PSALM 57:7

April 5

A girl can never have too many pairs of shoes,
or too many reasons to thank God.

September 27

Her attitude was as light-as-air—
she had given God all her care.

April 6

My constant boast is God.
I can never thank You enough!

PSALM 44:8

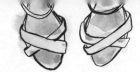

September 26

Help me to do Your will,
for You are my God.
Lead me in good paths,
for Your spirit is good.

PSALM 143:10

April 7

*She knew joy was one of her best accessories,
so she made up her mind to wear it every day.*

September 25

You are gifted—
and God used the infinite resources
of His goodness to create you.

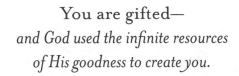

April 8

A happy face means a glad heart.

PROVERBS 15:13

September 24

What can we ever say to such
wonderful things as these?
If God is on our side,
who can ever be against us?

ROMANS 8:31

April 9

Chocolate, sweet chocolate...
let us never abandon the things
God has given us to enjoy.

September 23

Work hard and with gladness all the time...
doing the will of God with all your hearts.

EPHESIANS 6:7

April 10

Trust should be in the living God who always richly gives us all we need for our enjoyment.

1 TIMOTHY 6:17

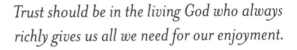

September 22

Put your heart into everything—
and see what God will do through you.

April 11

She started her day with a simple prayer,
"Lord, lead the way." Then she stepped out
the door with a heart full of courage.

September 21

You are good and do only good;
make me follow Your lead.

PSALM 119:68

April 12

Let me see Your kindness to me in the morning,
for I am trusting You. Show me where to walk,
for my prayer is sincere.

PSALM 143:8

September 20

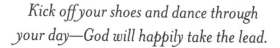

*Kick off your shoes and dance through
your day—God will happily take the lead.*

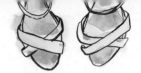

April 13

Love never goes out of style.

September 19

The Lord makes us strong!

PSALM 81:1

April 14

Let love guide your life.

COLOSSIANS 3:14

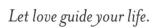

September 18

Cheer up!
Take courage if you are
depending on the Lord.

PSALM 31:24

April 15

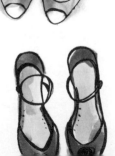

If we believe we can change the world,
God will show us how to do it!

September 17

She put on her rose-colored glasses and looked at everything through the eyes of faith— and her outlook was amazing.

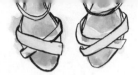

April 16

*You can get anything—**anything** you ask for in prayer—if you believe.*

MATTHEW 21:22

September 16

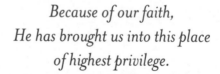

Because of our faith,
He has brought us into this place
of highest privilege.

ROMANS 5:2

April 17

A shoe sale is a great mood-lifter…
but it takes a good prayer to lift the spirit.

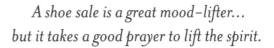

September 15

Is that a joyous choir I hear?
No, it is the Lord Himself
exulting over you in happy song.

ZEPHANIAH 3:18

April 18

Lord, You are my shield,
my glory, and my only hope.
You alone can lift my head.

PSALM 3:3

September 14

*Aren't you tickled pink
to be the joy of God's heart…
the reason for His happy song?*

April 19

Day Planners are great for organizing our days...but God is the only One who can organize our life.

September 13

Kind words are like honey—
enjoyable and healthful.

PROVERBS 16:24

April 20

*You saw me before I was born
and scheduled each day of my life
before I began to breathe.*

PSALM 139:16

September 12

Love forgets mistakes.

PROVERBS 17:9

April 21

The Lord will work out His plans for my life—
for Your loving-kindness, Lord,
continues forever.

PSALM 138:8

September 11

Remember the good—let go of the rest!

April 22

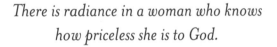

There is radiance in a woman who knows
how priceless she is to God.

September 10

*Your spiritual strength comes
as a gift from God.*

HEBREWS 13:9

April 23

You are precious to Me and honored,
and I love you.

ISAIAH 43:4

September 9

Look after each other so that not one of you
will fail to find God's best blessings.

HEBREWS 12:15

April 24

*A woman who fears and reverences God
shall be greatly praised.*

PROVERBS 31:30

September 8

A little black dress, a great hair style,
a flattering pair of heels—
just some of the things that make you feel like
the fabulous woman God created you to be!

April 25

If you can pray, you can conquer!

September 7

God blesses those who are kind.

PSALM 41:1

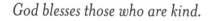

April 26

When I pray,
You answer me and encourage me
by giving me the strength I need.

PSALM 138:3

September 6

If God cares so wonderfully for flowers…
won't He more surely care for you?

MATTHEW 6:30

April 27

*She looked up and knew everything
was going to be more than O.K.—
it was going to work out perfectly.*

September 5

Make your life like a garden full of daisies...
bright and happy to be basking
in the Lord's care.

April 28

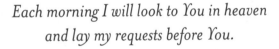

Each morning I will look to You in heaven
and lay my requests before You.

PSALM 5:3

September 4

*You have been with me from birth
and have helped me constantly—
no wonder I am always praising You!*

PSALM 71:6

April 29

God created every soul to sing.

September 3

I will tell everyone how good You are,
and of Your constant, daily care.

PSALM 71:15

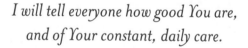

April 30

I sing His songs and
pray to God who gives me life.

PSALM 42:8

September 2

*The shoes matched her dress perfectly,
and she smiled, knowing God had put her
day together with the same attention to detail.*

May 1

*Faith is having the courage
to believe God will do it before we see it.*

September 1

We are able to hold our heads high no matter
what happens and know that all is well,
for we know how dearly God loves us.

ROMANS 5:5

May 2

What we hope for is waiting for us,
even though we cannot see it up ahead.

HEBREWS 11:1

August 31

Let your conversation
be gracious as well as sensible.

COLOSSIANS 4:6

May 3

*She was brave on the inside,
where God does great things...
and that's what mattered most.*

August 30

*Let the Spirit of God empower you
to face every challenge with style and grace.*

May 4

How we thank God for all of this!
It is He who makes us victorious through Jesus.

I CORINTHIANS 15:57

August 29

Be gentle and ready to forgive.

COLOSSIANS 3:13

May 5

If you will stir up this inner power,
you will never be afraid.

II TIMOTHY 1:8

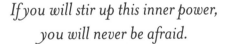

August 28

Put on gentleness like a favorite summer dress…
let it be an easy and comfortable
part of your life.

May 6

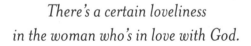

*There's a certain loveliness
in the woman who's in love with God.*

August 27

*Create in me a new,
clean heart, O God.*

PSALM 51:10

May 7

Praise her for the many fine things she does.
These good deeds of hers shall bring her honor.

PROVERBS 31:31

August 26

*I am radiant with joy
because of Your mercy.*

PSALM 31:7

May 8

Practice tenderhearted mercy
and kindness to others.

COLOSSIANS 3:12

August 25

*Glimpse at the beauty around you today—
it's nothing compared to the beauty within you.*

May 9

Love matters most.

August 24

You chart the path ahead of me,
and tell me where to stop and rest.

PSALM 139:3

May 10

In response to all He has done for us,
let us outdo each other
in being helpful and kind.

HEBREWS 10:24

August 23

How precious it is, Lord,
to realize that You are
thinking about me constantly!

PSALM 139:17

May 11

God has a plan for you today—
and it's good in every way.

August 22

A little pampering does a girl good—
you are delicately made
and precious to your Maker.

May 12

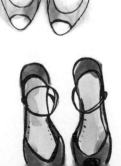

O Lord, my God...
we are ever in Your thoughts.

PSALM 40:5

August 21

Live one day at a time.

MATTHEW 6:34

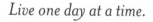

May 13

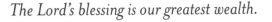

The Lord's blessing is our greatest wealth.

PROVERBS 10:22

August 20

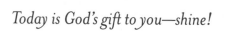

Today is God's gift to you—shine!

May 14

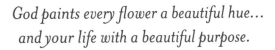

God paints every flower a beautiful hue…
and your life with a beautiful purpose.

August 19

Don't be afraid, for the Lord will go before you
and will be with you; He will not fail you.

DEUTERONOMY 31:8

May 15

He fulfills the desires
of those who reverence and trust Him.

PSALM 145:19

August 18

Face your day with a new sense of confidence—
God is with you!

May 16

She had a spring in her step,
God on her side,
and a fearless heart to face the day.

August 17

Those who turn many to righteousness
will glitter like the stars forever.

DANIEL 12:3

May 17

It is a wonderful thing to be alive!

ECCLESIASTES 11:7

August 16

Let Your favor shine again
upon Your servant.

PSALM 31:16

May 18

When the path ahead of us is washed away,
God will give us wings.

August 15

The graceful beauty of God shined on her…
as if she strolled through her day
under a spotlight from heaven.

May 19

Only God can see everything.

ECCLESIASTES 8:17

August 14

*Let everything He has made
give praise to Him.*

PSALM 148:5

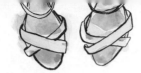

May 20

The Lord is faithful to His promises.
Blessed are all those who wait
for Him to help them.

ISAIAH 30:18

August 13

Head to toe,
you're exquisitely made.

May 21

*From a broken heel to a broken heart—
God cares.*

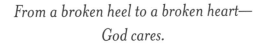

August 12

You want to be tools in the hands of God,
to be used for His good purposes.

ROMANS 6:13

May 22

The Lord still waits for You to come to Him,
so He can show you His love.

ISAIAH 30:18

August 11

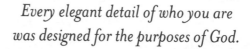

*Every elegant detail of who you are
was designed for the purposes of God.*

May 23

You are priceless to God.

August 10

Give Him first place in your life
and live as He wants you to.

MATTHEW 6:33

May 24

*The godly are able
to be generous with their gifts.*

PSALM 37:26

August 9

I chose you!
I appointed you to go and produce lovely fruit.

JOHN 15:16

May 25

God has given you something
you can give back to the world—
in a way no one else can.

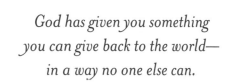

August 8

In God's eyes you are loved,
and you are lovely.

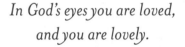

May 26

Give generously,
for your gifts will return to you later.

ECCLESIASTES 11:1

August 7

Don't hide your light!
Let it shine for all.

MATTHEW 5:15

May 27

Sand between your toes…
ocean breeze…blue sky…
glorious gifts from a generous God.

August 6

Shine your God-given light
on those around you today.

May 28

The earth belongs to God!
Everything in all the world is His!

PSALM 24:1

August 5

God gives those who please Him wisdom,
knowledge, and joy.

ECCLESIASTES 2:25

May 29

The heavens are telling the glory of God;
they are a marvelous display
of His craftsmanship.

PSALM 19:1

August 4

Live with joy!

May 30

*Lord,
make me all You want me to be!*

August 3

*We confidently and joyfully look forward
to actually becoming all that God
has had in mind for us to be.*

ROMANS 5:2

May 31

Don't be anxious about tomorrow.
God will take care of your tomorrow too.

MATTHEW 6:34

August 2

Let your dreams ignite your faith.

June 1

God cares about everything in your life
because He cares so much about you.

August 1

*Stir into flame the
strength and boldness that is in you.*

II TIMOTHY 1:6

June 2

You have always cared for me.

PSALM 4:1

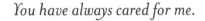

July 31

Step into each new day with the
boldness that only comes from God.

June 3

When we are kind, God smiles.

July 30

*I will bless the Lord and not forget
the glorious things He does for me.*

PSALM 103:2

June 4

Honor goes to kind and gracious women.

PROVERBS 11:16

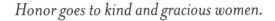

July 29

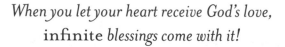

When you let your heart receive God's love,
infinite *blessings come with it!*

June 5

Anytime is a good time for a quiet prayer…
or dark chocolate.

July 28

There is nothing but goodness in Him!

PSALM 92:15

June 6

There is a right time for everything.

ECCLESIASTES 3:1

July 27

God is at work within you.

PHILIPPIANS 2:13

June 7

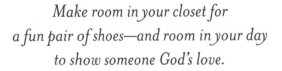

*Make room in your closet for
a fun pair of shoes—and room in your day
to show someone God's love.*

July 26

*God's love can be seen
in every circumstance.*

June 8

*If I had the gift of faith so that I could speak
to a mountain and make it move, I would
still be worth nothing at all without love.*

I CORINTHAINS 13:2

July 25

May God who gives patience,
steadiness, and encouragement
help you live in complete harmony.

ROMANS 15:5

June 9

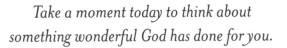

*Take a moment today to think about
something wonderful God has done for you.*

July 24

May you be given more and more of
God's kindness, peace, and love.

JUDE 1:2

June 10

Let all the joys of the godly
well up in praise to the Lord.

PSALM 33:1

July 23

*The sweetest thing God adds to life
is the gift of a trusted friend.*

June 11

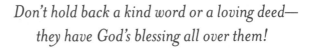

*Don't hold back a kind word or a loving deed—
they have God's blessing all over them!*

July 22

Thank You, Lord! How good You are!
Your love for us continues on forever.

PSALM 106:1

June 12

Day by day the Lord observes the
good deeds done by godly men,
and gives them eternal rewards.

PSALM 37:18

July 21

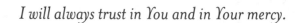

I will always trust in You and in Your mercy.

PSALM 13:5

June 13

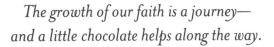

The growth of our faith is a journey—
and a little chocolate helps along the way.

July 20

*Lord, put my feet on the path You've chosen
for me, and let my heart be content.*

June 14

*I will praise the Lord
no matter what happens.*

PSALM 34:1

July 19

All God's words are right,
and everything He does is worthy of our trust.

PSALM 33:4

June 15

The best way to end a meal is with dessert...
and a day with prayer.

July 18

*Joy rises in my heart until I
burst out in songs of praise to Him.*

PSALM 28:7

June 16

*My only hope
is in Your love and faithfulness.*

PSALM 40:11

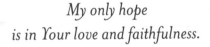

July 17

*Refresh your soul with hope—
let your spirit be filled with joy!*

June 17

*She wouldn't give up her
favorite pair of jeans, her passion for God,
or her determination to show the world
how one-of-a-kind she is.*

July 16

Every path He guides us on
is fragrant with His lovingkindness.

PSALM 25:10

June 18

Your workmanship is marvelous—
and how well I know it.

PSALM 139:14

July 15

You alone are my God.
My times are in Your hands.

PSALM 31:14

June 19

When we give our all to God,
He makes all things beautiful.

July 14

Let your day rest in God's hand,
and enjoy wherever it takes you!

June 20

Give yourselves humbly to God.

JAMES 4:7

July 13

We know how dearly God loves us,
and we feel His warm love everywhere.

ROMANS 5:5

June 21

*When you draw close to God,
God will draw close to you.*

JAMES 4:8

July 12

Your steadfast love, O Lord,
is as great as all the heavens.
Your faithfulness reaches beyond the clouds.

PSALM 36:5

June 22

*God's plan for your life
is as special as you are.*

July 11

Being trendy is fun, she thought,
but there was an incredible comfort
in knowing God's love for her
would never change.

June 23

You both precede and follow me,
and place Your hand of blessing on my head.

PSALM 139:5

July 10

My protection and success
come from God alone.

PSALM 62:7

June 24

*Every girl needs a cute purse, red shoes,
and a good place to be alone with God.*

July 9

Whatever God says to us
is full of living power.

HEBREWS 4:12

June 25

Let us go right in,
to God Himself,
with true hearts fully trusting
Him to receive us.

HEBREWS 10:22

July 8

If God says it, trust it.

June 26

The one thing I want from God,
the thing I seek most of all, is the privilege of…
living in His presence every day of my life.

PSALM 27:4

July 7

Be delighted with the Lord.
Then He will give you all your heart's desires.

PSALM 37:4

June 27

*Girlfriends are an essential part
of God's goodness to us.*

July 6

Just tell me what to do and I will do it, Lord.
As long as I live I'll wholeheartedly obey.

PSALM 119:33, 34

June 28

Whatever is good and perfect
comes to us from God.

JAMES 1:17

July 5

She wanted to grow in beauty and grace,
so she asked God to show her the seeds
she should plant in the soil of her heart.

June 29

*Chocolate is proof that God is
sensitive to our needs...
and meets each one perfectly.*

July 4

He is the strength of my heart;
He is mine forever!

PSALM 73:26

June 30

*Many blessings are given
to those who trust the Lord.*

PSALM 40:4

July 3

She was full of joy and generosity,
and everyone knew
her heart belonged to God.

July 1

*Life is adorned with
the beauty of God's blessings.*

July 2

Lord,
You have poured out amazing blessings!

PSALM 85:1